Navigating Global Transition Again

A JOURNEY OF FAITH

GRADUATE PLANNER
2ND EDITION

JENI WARD & KATH WILLIAMS

Interwoven

Second Edition 2024

ISBN paperback: 978-0-6457886-0-0

This edition was published in Aberfoyle Park by Mission Interlink in April 2024

Illustrations by:
River by Emma Elliot page 10
Artwork © Lorien Illustrations 2017. www.lorien-illustrations.com. Scripture is from the ESV®Bible (The Holy Bible, English Standard Version®),copyright © 2001 by Crossway Bibles, a publishing ministry of Good News Publishers. Used by permission. All rights reserved.
Bible passage reference NET Bible ® Copyright
Colouring pages 40 & 56
Zeborah Grace: Colouring page 84
Typesetting by: Kath Williams
Cover layout by
With publication assistance from Immortalise

Bible passage reference NET Bible ® Copyright

Forward

When big changes in life hit, life gets overwhelming. There is a flood of unfamiliarity, and in the midst of that chaos we have to make decisions – often life-changing decisions. These seasons of transition are stressful, uncomfortable, and quite often turning points we'll look back on.

I don't know about you, but I've often wished someone could just tell me what to do. Not make all my decisions for me, but just – make it a bit easier! Calm the   chaos, make order from the maelstrom of emotions and overwhelm.

In nearly twenty years working with teens and twenty from around the world who grew up outside their passport countries, I have heard hundreds of stories. Stories of their lives, their joys, their struggles, their journeys, their successes. One thing almost all of them had in common was one of their most difficult seasons of change: finishing high school. The most difficult of all? Moving to live in their passport country. For a good chunk of TCKs, these two experiences overlap. No, they don't just overlap – they collide.

In the midst of the emotional and practical chaos of such a big season of transition, we can't keep track of everything. That is why this book is so important. It provides a comprehensive framework to scaffold one of the most difficult experiences of TCK life: finishing high school and moving away.

There are things in this book you will no doubt think are obvious. Great! This workbook will remind you to get working on them – and perhaps earlier than you would on your own. It paces out all the aspects of leaving well so you have time to fit everything in. Most importantly, it doesn't stop when you wave goodbye and get on that plane but continues with you into that first week after arriving, when all is chaos. It checks in with you a few months later, and guides you through that whole first year.

Seasons of transition are stressful. We often choose to tune out, to turn off, to ignore the stress and hope it goes away. Processing our stress is much more valuable, but it can feel so hard to do. The Graduate Transition Planner makes it easy. You still have to show up and do the work, but the steps have been laid out for you – all you need do is follow. What a gift.

I hope you embrace this gift, not only the book you are reading, but this whole season of life. As you process everything you go through, I hope you find peace in knowing others have trod this path ahead of you. You're entering a time of life that can be stressful, but you aren't alone in it.
Tanya Crossman - Author of Misunderstood

ENDORSEMENTS

"Transitioning to a new culture can be a daunting experience for young people. Navigating Global Transition Again is a unique tool that can make the process less challenging and more meaningful. It is designed to be easy to follow as they enter their passport country, which they may not know much about and may not even consider their home. The authors have poured their experience, thought, and love into this guidebook, making it an invaluable resource for any Third Culture Kid (TCK). This guidebook offers hope and a sense of safety during a significant spiritual and physical transition."

Nataliya Osipova, National Director of Australian Evangelical Alliance,
Member of the WEA Global Leadership Council for Mission Commission.

"As someone who grew up as a Third Culture Kid (TCK) and is now a father to TCKs, as well as a principal to TCKs, I strongly endorse this resource as an invaluable guide for graduating students who are about to embark on another transition to university. Starting tertiary education can be an incredibly daunting step, but this resource is specifically designed to help TCKs not just survive the transition, but also thrive in it. I would like to extend a heartfelt thanks to the authors for their meticulous research and thoughtful care in creating this resource for our beloved TCKs."

James Bellingham, Executive Principal of 3H School International

"Navigating Global Transitions Again is so much more than a practical planner for graduating TCKs: it's a two-year guide to help you transition emotionally and spiritually to your passport country. Full of thoughtful journal/discussion prompts and memory-stirring activities, it helps you track your emotions in your final year abroad, lays out the practical steps to take to transition to your passport country, and continues the journey through the first full year of repatriation".

Elizabeth Trotter, author of Serving Well:
Help for the Wannabe, Newbie, or Weary Cross-cultural Worker,
Editor-in-chief of the missions website A Life Overseas.

Transition can be a difficult time for anyone working cross cultural, but especially for young adults, who are not only traversing a new cultural experience but working out who they are as an adult, their interests, passions, and where they belong. That's why this planner is so important.

Navigating Global Transitions Again, scaffolds a reflective experience, prompting the young adult to look back and look forward. This works also as a practical tool for equipping parents and mentors to guide their young person during this time of transition and change, which will be different to their own re-entry experience.

Jane Fairweather
Personnel Director – Interserve Australia

Acknowledgements

We are so thankful that God has given us the opportunity to be involved in this project.

Many thanks to all of those who have contributed; Mission Interlink, Interserve Australia and SIM Australia for giving us the margin to make this collaboration possible. Also, to our families who have supported, encouraged, and provided childcare. We also want to thank all those people that work alongside TCKS.

Thank you to Ben from Immortalise publishing for editing our book and giving us extra feedback.

Thank you to Frances Early for your contribution to the 1st Edition of the book.

Contents

NAVIGATING GLOBAL TRANSITION AGAIN

About us

INTERWOVEN

Interwoven is a Missions Interlink Ministry build through a partnership between workers from SIM Australia and Interserve Australia who have a heart to see Missionary Kids physically, spiritually, and mentally thrive on the mission field. Our primary focus is developing materials that speak directly to Missionary Kids; however, we would also like to be a support and resource for those who work with and love Missionary Kids.

KATH WILLIAMS (ISV AUSTRALIA)

I am a "TCK wannabe." I grew up in Australia and have only moved three times in my whole life. I am a qualified social worker and became passionate about working with TCKs after helping at a team retreat for a mission organisation. I came to realise after, that throughout my youth, I had friends who were Missionary Kids and how much I valued their friendship. After coming back from the team retreat, I started to ask questions about what was needed to support these young people as they returned to their passport countries and how we can help them find their identity in Christ. In 2016, I headed to Cambodia where I worked with an International school and helped at the international youth group to have a better understanding of TCKs. Since coming back to Australia, my passion is to see TCKs well cared for and looked after and for organizations to do member care well. Interwoven is a passion of mine to see mission agencies work together to bring the focus of the Gospel and to see these children and young people well cared for.

JENI WARD (SIM AUSTRALIA)

I am so glad that this resource has found you. Being a TCK who had two TCKs as parents I feel like I have come by my Third Culture identification honestly. My own experience has been a blend of incredible experiences and struggles, much like anyone else's. One of my most distinct memories was the first time someone in my life taught the Gospel like it was a message for me. I had heard it, sung it, and recited it my whole life. I think it was assumed that I had got the message that God's love was for me simply by the environment I lived in. But I really hadn't. It wasn't until a teacher took the time to teach the Bible like it was for my very soul and not just a tool for ministry. My prayer is that this might be a tool that will meet TCKs in the same way. God knows you, sees you, and loves you. Beloved of God the Gospel is for you!

Introduction

Dear Graduate,

As you enter your final year, here is a tool to help you prepare for the big changes to come in your life. There may be some hard moments but there will be some things to celebrate as well. This planner can help you ask questions and seek out support as you enter the next stage of life as you prepare to leave and as you enter your new country.

This is what each section has:
-Practical- This is where you can think through questions in regard to the move and make some decisions on the next step to take.
-Heart- Is intended for you to share with someone how you are feeling about the move and discuss them.
-Reflection- Takes you on a study throughout Galatians.
-Thoughts and Plans- Give you an option to write down any plans or thoughts that you would like to process as you go along this journey.
-To do list- is for you to write down things you may need to accomplish that month.
-Mood Tracker- Is to track how you are going emotional.
Activities in which you can do.
-Wreck this Journal Page- This is an opportunity to create it as unique as you that means you can add photos, deface the page, colour outside. It is up to you.
-Don't be limited if you run out of space just add more pages.
-Do it in your own time there is no race.
-Feel free to read ahead and think about what is coming.
-Hash-tag us if you want in some of your pictures at #interwoven
- Bridging person- Is some one from your passport country who you can walk alongside with. Ask those questions you want too.

This is your planner make it your own.

You can walk through this planner by yourself, alongside your family or with your class-mates. We recommend finding a bridging person in the country you are moving too. This person is to help you understand the culture. They should be feel comfortable with asking any questions that come to mind.

Mood Tracker

A mood tracker is part of your planner that allows you to track whether you are feeling happy, sad, tired, angry, bored, etc.

Blue- Sad

Red- Angry

Yellow – Happy

Green- Anxious

Orange- Worried

Purple- Scared

Add your own code

Reflection Introduction

As you start on the journey with Navigating Global Transition again, we are going to take you through the book of Galatians. It's your choice how you interact with it, how you answer the questions or how much you do. Each month there is a reflection with a passage from Galatians and a question for you to consider as you process your transition.

Galatians is a book found in the New Testament, it was a letter written from Paul to a number of early Christians in Galatia. Galatians region had been a Roman province since 189 BC and Paul had worked hard on his first missionary journey to found many churches in the region, including Antioch, Derbe, Iconium, and Lystra. The main purpose of the book is to put an end to the false teachings of the Judaizers. This letter was written to remind Jesus' followers to embrace the message that is given through the life and teaching of Christ and it justifies all people through faith and empowers them to live like Jesus called them to.

The River

The river is a tool which you will use throughout the planner. The river is your processing self reflection-tool to reflect where you are at in and how you are coping along the way.

On one side of the river is the place you are currently and the other side is the place you are going this could be your passport country. The river is where you process your transition. In there you can feel like your drowning. What are the supports that are keeping you up? Do you feel like you are still in the middle of the river or on the shore.

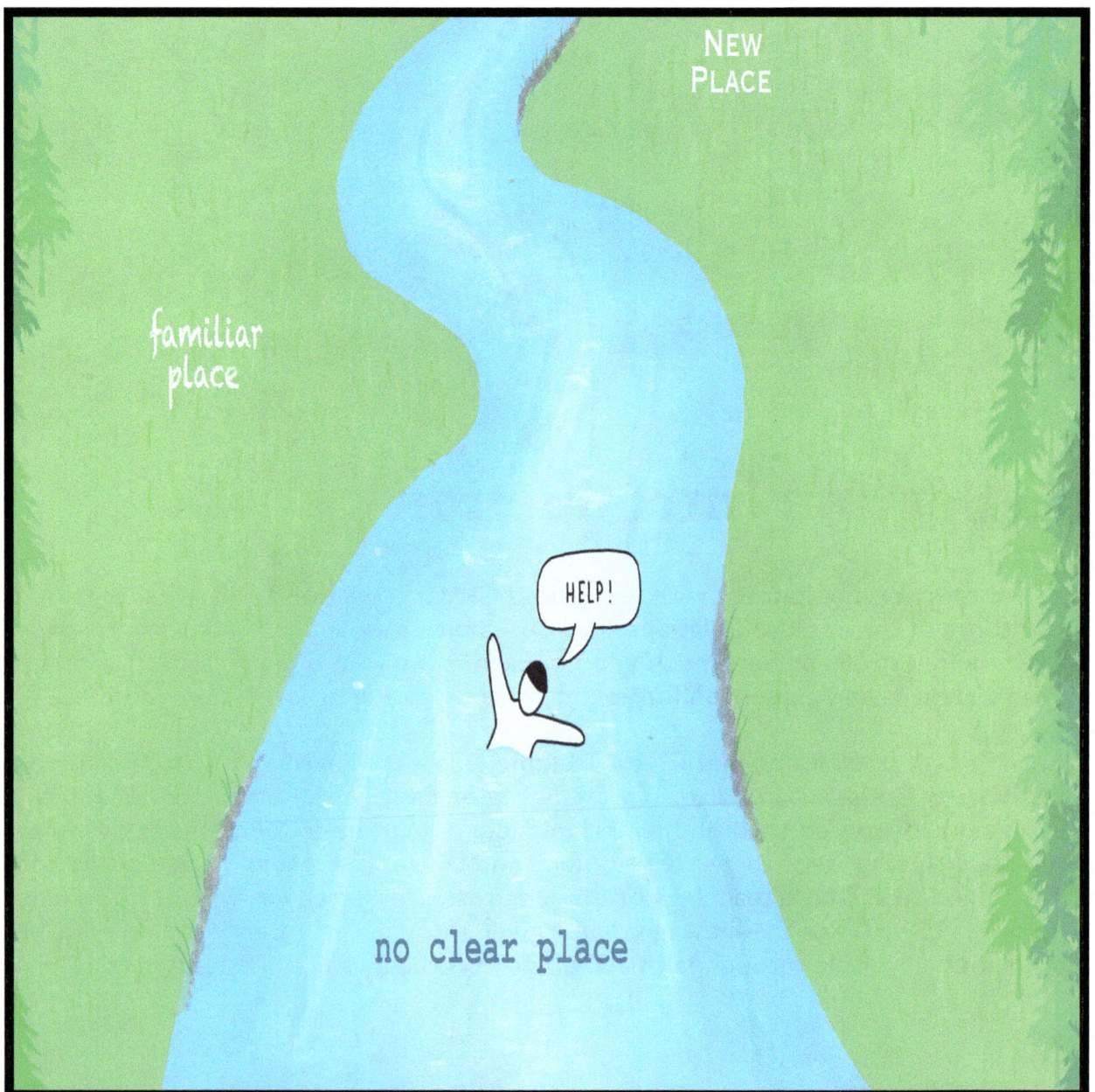

NEW PLACE

familiar place

HELP!

no clear place

Donovan (1991) A model of major transition

NOTES:

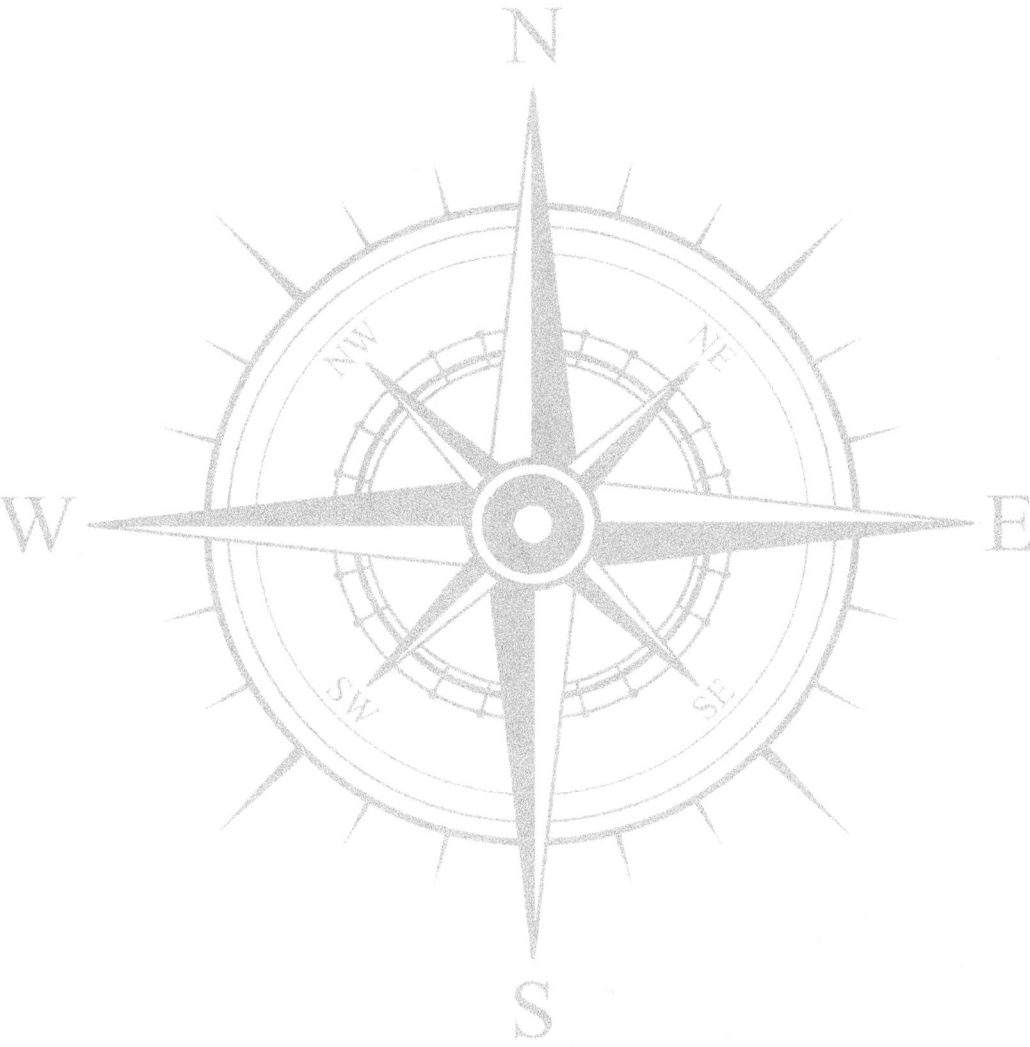

Important dates & Birthdays

January

February

March

April

May

June

July

August

September

October

November

December

Contacts

Name	Socials	Phone

12 Months Ahead

Practical

THINK

- [ ] What are you planning for the coming year?
- [ ] Do you need to apply for scholarships?
- [ ] Is there financial aid available for you?
- [ ] Do you need to learn to cook or clean?

DECIDE

- [ ] Who is your bridging person?
- [ ] What meals do you want to learn to cook?

Heart

SHARE

- [ ] How do you feel about leaving?
- [ ] How do you feel about where you are going?
- [ ] What are you concerned about?
- [ ] What are you looking forward to?

DISCUSS

- [ ] What do you want to do before you go?
- [ ] Who do you want to spend your final year with?

TO DO:

- [ ]
- [ ]
- [ ]
- [ ]
- [ ]
- [ ]
- [ ]
- [ ]

MOOD TRACKER

- [ ] Week 1
- [ ] Week 2
- [ ] Week 3
- [ ] Week 4
- [ ] Week 5
- [ ] Week 6
- [ ] Week 7
- [ ] Week 8
- [ ] Week 9
- [ ] Week 10
- [ ] Week 11
- [ ] Week 12

THOUGHTS AND PLANS

_____

_____

_____

_____

_____

_____

_____

_____

_____

_____

_____

_____

REFLECTION

Because of your parents' ministry, people probably assumed you are Christians, as your parents are. Paul states that the gospel he preaches is not of human origin but it is what he has received from Jesus Christ. You may have a relationship with God or you may not, but wherever you find yourself on your faith journey, this conversation is for you. This first month asks the question: what do you believe in?

As a TCK, have you ever felt that you had to please people? Do you feel your faith needs to be justified? This is a journey for you, it's a struggle with God. If you haven't wrestled yet with God or you are in the midst of working out where you stand, this is an invitation to come to Christ as you are and trust him with this journey.

BIBLE PASSAGE

GALATIANS 1:1-12

From Paul, an apostle (not from men, nor by human agency, but by Jesus Christ and God the Father who raised him from the dead) 2 and all the brothers with me, to the churches of Galatia.

3 Grace and peace to you from God the Father and our Lord Jesus Christ, 4 who gave himself for our sins to rescue us from this present evil age according to the will of our God and Father, 5 to whom be glory forever and ever! Amen.

6 I am astonished that you are so quickly deserting the one who called you by the grace of Christ and are following a different gospel— 7 not that there really is another gospel, but there are some who are disturbing you and wanting to distort the gospel of Christ. 8 But even if we (or an angel from heaven) should preach a gospel contrary to the one we preached to you, let him be condemned to hell! 9 As we have said before, and now I say again, if any one is preaching to you a gospel contrary to what you received, let him be condemned to hell! 10 Am I now trying to gain the approval of people, or of God? Or am I trying to please people? If I were still trying to please people, I would not be a slave of Christ!

11 Now I want you to know, brothers and sisters, that the gospel I preached is not of human origin. 12 For I did not receive it or learn it from any human source; instead I received it by a revelation of Jesus Christ.

QUESTIONS

• What do you believe in?

• Have you felt pressured to please people over God?

• When Paul met God on the road to Damascus it completely changed his life.

• Read Acts 9:1-31.

• What did God say to Paul?

NOTES:

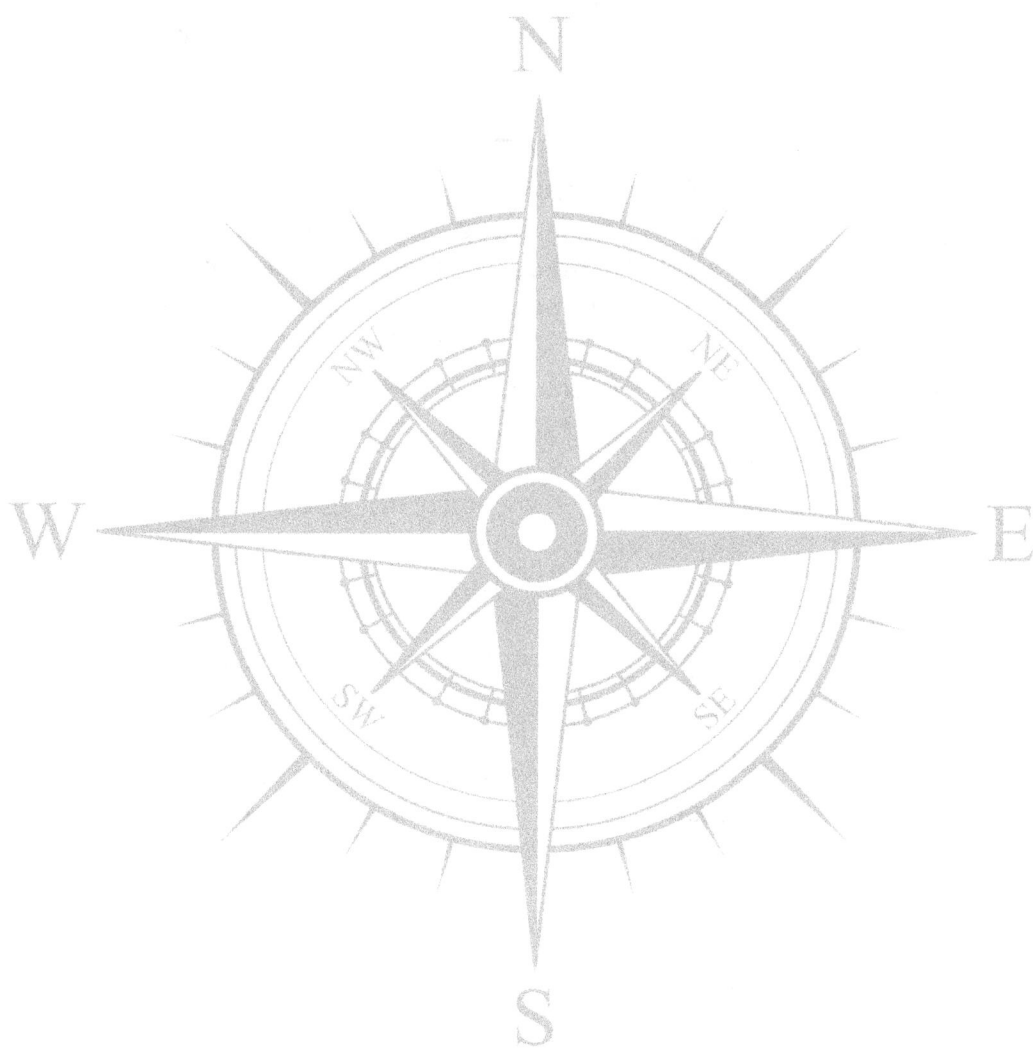

Photo Scavenger Hunt

INSTRUCTIONS:

Photo scavenger hunts are a fun way to revisit favourite spots and dwell literally or mentally on important memories. You can do this hunt all together as a group of friends or split into teams or with your family and make it a little more competitive. Either way, it's best to give yourself a time limit and an idea of what you will do at the end (e.g.. go out to eat, get ice-cream and review the pictures at home, etc.).

A FEW RULES:

Don't take the prompts literally. You can take photos in spots that remind you of the memory in the prompt it doesn't have to be the actual place. You can walk or drive but, if possible, take each photo in a different place.

- You can take selfies, ask other people to be in the photo or ask other people to take the photo for you.
- You should take each photo as a group.
- It's best to stage a scene in each photo to remind you of what you did or felt during this memory. Each person can play themselves or you can switch roles (e.g. If you remember going bungee jumping you might pose yourselves   screaming as you pretend to fly through the air over a creek).
- You can hash-tag us #interwoven so we can see the experience
-

TAKE A PHOTO THAT REMINDS YOU OF:

- A fun holiday you took together.
- Something you did that you never want to do again.
- A memorable airport experience.
- The first place you lived overseas as a family.
- A favourite restaurant.
- Your most interesting food experience.
- A place that amazed you.
- The first place you met some close friends.
- A weird place or experience you never want to forget.
- A place you always wanted to go but never had the chance.
- A really great time with friends.
- A happy reunion.
- A disgusting experience.
- Something embarrassing.
- A time you felt close.
- A favourite cultural experience.
- A time you got a big surprise.
- A time when someone had to go to the hospital.
- Something funny that happened overseas.
- A family disaster.
- A place that feels safe.
- The transport you were on

Pictures of where you live

9 Months Ahead

Practical

THINK

- [ ] What do you want to take with you and what do you want to leave behind?
- [ ] Make a list of your favourite places.
- [ ] What are your travel arrangements?

DECIDE

- [ ] What do you want to have memories of?

Heart

SHARE

- [ ] How do you feel about leaving?
- [ ] How do you feel about where you are going?
- [ ] What are you concerned about?
- [ ] What are you looking forward to?

DISCUSS

- [ ] What are some of the things you would like to do when you enter your new country?

TO DO:

- [ ]
- [ ]
- [ ]
- [ ]
- [ ]
- [ ]
- [ ]
- [ ]

MOOD TRACKER

- [ ] Week 1
- [ ] Week 2
- [ ] Week 3
- [ ] Week 4
- [ ] Week 5
- [ ] Week 6
- [ ] Week 7
- [ ] Week 8
- [ ] Week 9
- [ ] Week 10
- [ ] Week 11
- [ ] Week 12

THOUGHTS AND PLANS

_____

_____

_____

_____

_____

_____

_____

_____

_____

_____

_____

REFLECTION

Who does God belong to? This is a question that you may have come across while living in a cross-cultural world. Is he a God of the West?

Was he packaged and brought to different parts of the world through colonialism? This can be the message that is presented in our current global conversation.

But what is Paul saying in this passage? He is reminding the believers in Galatia that God is the one who is writing the story. He is the one who is sending out his message. Being someone who is working in service of the word of God is not a position of power, but one of humility.

BIBLE PASSAGE

GALATIANS 1:21- 2:3

For you have heard of my former way of life in Judaism, how I was savagely persecuting the church of God and trying to destroy it. 14 I was advancing in Judaism beyond many of my contemporaries in my nation, and was extremely zealous for the traditions of my ancestors. 15 But when the one who set me apart from birth and called me by his grace was pleased 16 to reveal his Son in me so that I could preach him among the Gentiles, I did not go to ask advice from any human being, 17 nor did I go up to Jerusalem to see those who were apostles before me, but right away I departed to Arabia, and then returned to Damascus.

18 Then after three years I went up to Jerusalem to visit Cephas and get information from him, and I stayed with him fifteen days. 19 But I saw none of the other apostles except James the Lord's brother. 20 I assure you that, before God, I am not lying about what I am writing to you! 21 Afterward I went to the regions of Syria and Cilicia. 22 But I was personally unknown to the churches of Judea that are in Christ. 23 They were only hearing, "The one who once persecuted us is now proclaiming the good news of the faith he once tried to destroy." 24 So they glorified God because of me.

Confirmation from the Jerusalem Apostles

2 Then after fourteen years I went up to Jerusalem again with Barnabas, taking Titus along too. 2 I went there because of a revelation and presented to them the gospel that I preach among the Gentiles. But I did so only in a private meeting with the influential people, to make sure that I was not running—or had not run—in vain. 3 Yet not even Titus, who was with me, was compelled to be circumcised, although he was a Greek.

QUESTIONS

• What does it mean to have Jesus revealed to you?'

• Have you seen God totally change someone's life?

• Where do you turn when you are unsure if you are doing the right thing?

NOTES:

Pictures of your favourite restaurants

Pictures of important people in your life

6 Months Ahead

Practical

THINK

- ☐ What will you do in an emergency?
- ☐ Make a list of people with whom you want to spend time before you go.
- ☐ What are some habits you can start now to have family connection?

DECIDE

- ☐ Are all your travel documents up to date?
- ☐ What documents do you need to take with you? E.g. birth certificates, ID papers
- ☐ Make a travel pack

Heart

SHARE

- ☐ How do you feel about leaving?
- ☐ How do you feel about where you are going?
- ☐ What are you concerned about?
- ☐ What are you looking forward to?

DISCUSS

- ☐ What do you want to do before you go?
- ☐ What does your family think about your plan?

TO DO:

- ☐
- ☐
- ☐
- ☐
- ☐
- ☐
- ☐
- ☐

MOOD TRACKER

- ☐ Week 1
- ☐ Week 2
- ☐ Week 3
- ☐ Week 4
- ☐ Week 5
- ☐ Week 6
- ☐ Week 7
- ☐ Week 8
- ☐ Week 9
- ☐ Week 10
- ☐ Week 11
- ☐ Week 12

THOUGHTS AND PLANS

_____

_____

_____

_____

_____

_____

_____

_____

_____

_____

_____

_____

REFLECTION

When someone talks about culture there are probably a lot of things that come to mind for you. What is the culture that your parents come from? What clothing, language, and activities are considered acceptable or unacceptable to them. What about the context you have lived in for the last year? What are the differences that you have seen? Where do you feel like you fit in the conversation or culture?

Paul is writing in this passage to a group of believers who were struggling with how much of their cultural and religious laws should be applied to their lives as believers. Using the specific example of circumcision Paul shows that believers are no longer under the law of custom and culture, though they may live in respect of it by their own choice, but their walk with God is under grace. God It is not the following of laws that make a way to salvation, but the grace that God has freely given.

Are there laws from your family, school, or the cultures you have lived in and among that you feel you need to abide by in order to be acceptable to God? Are there requirements that you have been trying to meet that feel impossible. Gods grace is over all these things. You don't have to be perfect to be a believer. God just asks for you. Can you meet Him in this place?

BIBLE PASSAGE

GALATIANS 2:4-21

Now this matter arose because of the false brothers with false pretences who slipped in unnoticed to spy on our freedom that we have in Christ Jesus, to make us slaves. 5 But we did not surrender to them even for a moment, in order that the truth of the gospel would remain with you.

6 But from those who were influential (whatever they were makes no difference to me; God shows no favouritism between people)—those influential leaders added nothing to my message. 7 On the contrary, when they saw that I was entrusted with the gospel to the uncircumcised just as Peter was entrusted with the gospel to the circumcised 8 (for he who empowered Peter for his apostleship to the circumcised also empowered me for my apostleship to the Gentiles) 9 and when James, Cephas, and John, who had a reputation as pillars, recognized the grace that had been given to me, they gave to Barnabas and me the right hand of fellowship, agreeing that we would go to the Gentiles and they to the circumcised. 10 They requested only that we remember the poor, the very thing I also was eager to do.

11 But when Cephas came to Antioch, I opposed him to his face, because he had clearly done wrong. 12 Until certain people came from James, he had been eating with the Gentiles. But when they arrived, he stopped doing this and separated himself because he was afraid of those who were pro-circumcision. 13 And the rest of the Jews also joined with him in this hypocrisy, so that even Barnabas was led astray with them by their hypocrisy. 14 But when I saw that they were not behaving consistently with the truth of the gospel, I said to Cephas in front of them all, "If you, although you are a Jew, live like a Gentile and not like a Jew, how can you try to force the Gentiles to live like Jews?"

15 We are Jews by birth and not Gentile sinners, 16 yet we know that no one is justified by the works of the law but by the faithfulness of Jesus Christ. And we have come to believe in Christ Jesus, so that we may be justified by the faithfulness of Christ and not by the works of the law, because by the works of the law no one will be justified. 17 But if while seeking to be justified in Christ we ourselves have also been found to be sinners, is Christ then one who encourages sin? Absolutely not! 18 But if I build up again those things I once destroyed, I demonstrate that I am one who breaks God's law. 19 For through the law I died to the law so that I may live to God. 20 I have been crucified with Christ, and it is no longer I who live, but Christ lives in me. So the life I now live in the body, I live because of the faithfulness of the Son of God, who loved me and gave himself for me. 21 I do not set aside God's grace, because if righteousness could come through the law, then Christ died for nothing!

QUESTIONS

• What does it mean to preserve the truth of the Gospel?

• What does it mean for God to 'work through someone?

• How have you seen God working in different ways?

NOTES:

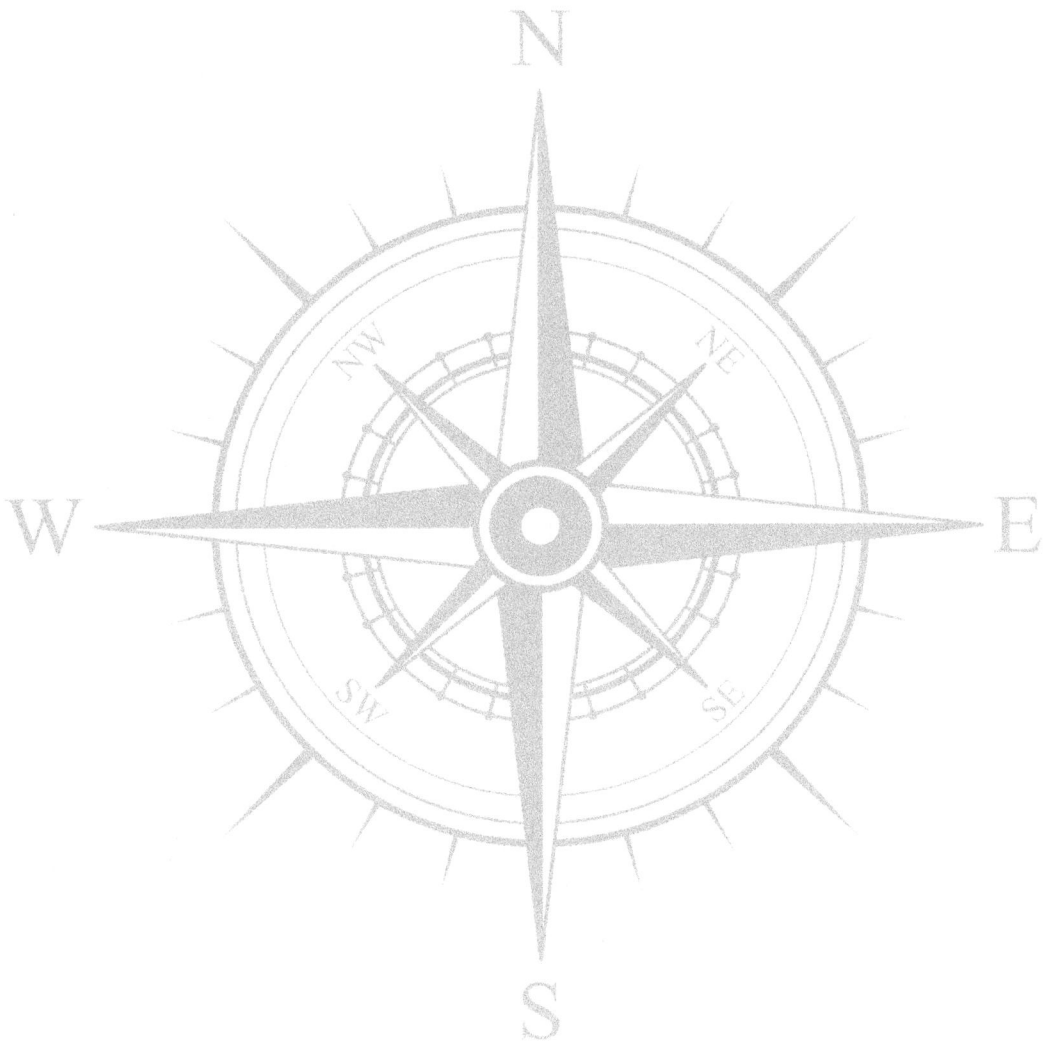

Write out your favourite phrases or slang from your country

Pictures of your favourite spots

3 Months Ahead

Practical

THINK

- [ ] What do you plan to do for income?
- [ ] Start planning days with special people in your life.
- [ ] Are there people with whom you need to reconcile?

DECIDE

- [ ] Who can write a reference for future employment?
- [ ] Start sorting what you will take with you and what you will leave behind.
- [ ] Do you need to purchase gifts to take with you?

Heart

SHARE

- [ ] How do you feel about leaving?
- [ ] How do you feel about where you are going?
- [ ] What are you concerned about?
- [ ] What are you looking forward to?

DISCUSS

- [ ] How will you continue your friendships through this transition?
- [ ] How will you keep in contact?

TO DO:

- [ ]
- [ ]
- [ ]
- [ ]
- [ ]
- [ ]
- [ ]
- [ ]

MOOD TRACKER

- [ ] Week 1
- [ ] Week 2
- [ ] Week 3
- [ ] Week 4

THOUGHTS AND PLANS

_____

_____

_____

_____

_____

_____

_____

_____

_____

_____

_____

REFLECTION

So what is faith? You may even have a convenient memorised answer that you have used many times before, but what has it looked like when you have seen it lived out? Believers are supposed to live out their faith by sharing it with others, but you can try so hard and still feel like you fail. You can try so hard to be what you think you should be, but run out of strength and ability before you meet the mark you have set. Paul reminds the Galatians that they simply cannot do this walk under their own strength. They need the Holy Spirit not just as a support to their own purposes, but as the guide and director of their steps. Jesus told the disciples that it was better for them that He leave and the Holy Spirit come and walk with them (John 16:7).

It is no minor support role that the Holy Spirit plays in you being able to live in the grace God has given. Living in your own strength can make things substantially harder. It sucks to try and strive toward an unreachable goal. Believers need to do it as a children of God with His Spirit beside them. God invites people to be comfortable with who they are and see themselves as a child of God. God is not afraid of human messiness or the things that need to be worked though in a person's life. He is there for you as you are!

BIBLE PASSAGE

GALATIANS 3:1-9

You foolish Galatians! Who has cast a spell on you? Before your eyes Jesus Christ was vividly portrayed as crucified! 2 The only thing I want to learn from you is this: Did you receive the Spirit by doing the works of the law or by believing what you heard? 3 Are you so foolish? Although you began with the Spirit, are you now trying to finish by human effort? 4 Have you suffered so many things for nothing?—If indeed it was for nothing. 5 Does God then give you the Spirit and work miracles among you by your doing the works of the law or by your believing what you heard?

6 Just as Abraham believed God, and it was credited to him as righteousness, 7 so then, understand that those who believe are the sons of Abraham. 8 And the scripture, foreseeing that God would justify the Gentiles by faith, proclaimed the gospel to Abraham ahead of time, saying, "All the nations will be blessed in you." 9 So then those who believe are blessed along with Abraham the believer.

QUESTIONS

• Why did the Galatians receive the Holy Spirit?

• What is faith?

• If this is true for all who have faith in Jesus, what does that mean for building relationships with believers from other cultures?

NOTES:

Make a packaging collage of your favourite labels

Recipes of your favourite food

2 Months Ahead

Practical

THINK

- ☐ Who do you want to be present for your departure and arrival?
- ☐ What will you use for transport at your new location?
- ☐ What practical gear will you need at your new place?

DECIDE

- ☐ How do you want to say goodbye? E.g. party, event, church
- ☐ Plan your goodbyes.

Heart

SHARE

- ☐ How do you feel about leaving?
- ☐ How do you feel about where you are going?
- ☐ What are you concerned about?
- ☐ What are you looking forward to?

DISCUSS

- ☐ How do you say, "No," in a culturally appropriate way?
- ☐ What are some boundaries you have established that you want to keep as you move?
- ☐ Mark where you sit currently on the river diagram.

TO DO:

- ☐
- ☐
- ☐
- ☐
- ☐
- ☐
- ☐
- ☐

MOOD TRACKER

☐ Week 1

☐ Week 2

☐ Week 3

☐ Week 4

THOUGHTS AND PLANS

_____

_____

_____

_____

_____

_____

_____

_____

_____

_____

REFLECTION

Have you lived in a place where you struggle to make sense of the laws and politics in your context? This is a very common human experience. There are also times when you may move from a context where you were comfortable with the laws into a place where everything is different. It can be a lot to process and the new laws can feel like nonsense to your logic. This is the human world that we live in. But God invites us into a life of freedom through a relationship with him that is not under the law. A freedom where no one is discounted by the judgement of people or their sins, but made acceptable by the love of God.

It is true that within the church there are plenty of examples of judgemental people being held to laws of context, culture, and history. As you anticipate your upcoming move, have you recognised God's voice of love and freedom above the voices of broken brothers and sisters?

If you find yourself in a moment of doubt, take a look at the life of Abraham. God chose him, and kept choosing him, to show His love even though he was messy and messed up.

BIBLE PASSAGE

GALATIANS 3:10-22

10 For all who rely on doing the works of the law are under a curse because it is written, "Cursed is everyone who does not keep on doing everything written in the book of the law." 11 Now it is clear no one is justified before God by the law because the righteous one will live by faith. 12 But the law is not based on faith, but the one who does the works of the law will live by them. 13 Christ redeemed us from the curse of the law by becoming a curse for us (because it is written, "Cursed is everyone who hangs on a tree") 14 in order that in Christ Jesus the blessing of Abraham would come to the Gentiles, so that we could receive the promise of the Spirit by faith.

Inheritance Comes from Promises and not Law

15 Brothers and sisters, I offer an example from everyday life: When a covenant has been ratified, even though it is only a human contract, no one can set it aside or add anything to it. 16 Now the promises were spoken to Abraham and to his descendant. Scripture does not say, "and to the descendants," referring to many, but "and to your descendant," referring to one, who is Christ. 17 What I am saying is this: The law that came 430 years later does not cancel a covenant previously ratified by God, so as to invalidate the promise. 18 For if the inheritance is based on the law, it is no longer based on the promise, but God graciously gave it to Abraham through the promise.

19 Why then was the law given? It was added because of transgressions, until the arrival of the descendant to whom the promise had been made. It was administered through angels by an intermediary. 20 Now an intermediary is not for one party alone, but God is one. 21 Is the law therefore opposed to the promises of God? Absolutely not! For if a law had been given that was able to give life, then righteousness would certainly have come by the law. 22 But the scripture imprisoned everything under sin so that the promise could be given—because of the faithfulness of Jesus Christ—to those who believe.

QUESTIONS

• Reflect and Discuss

• What does it mean to believe in Jesus Christ?

NOTES:

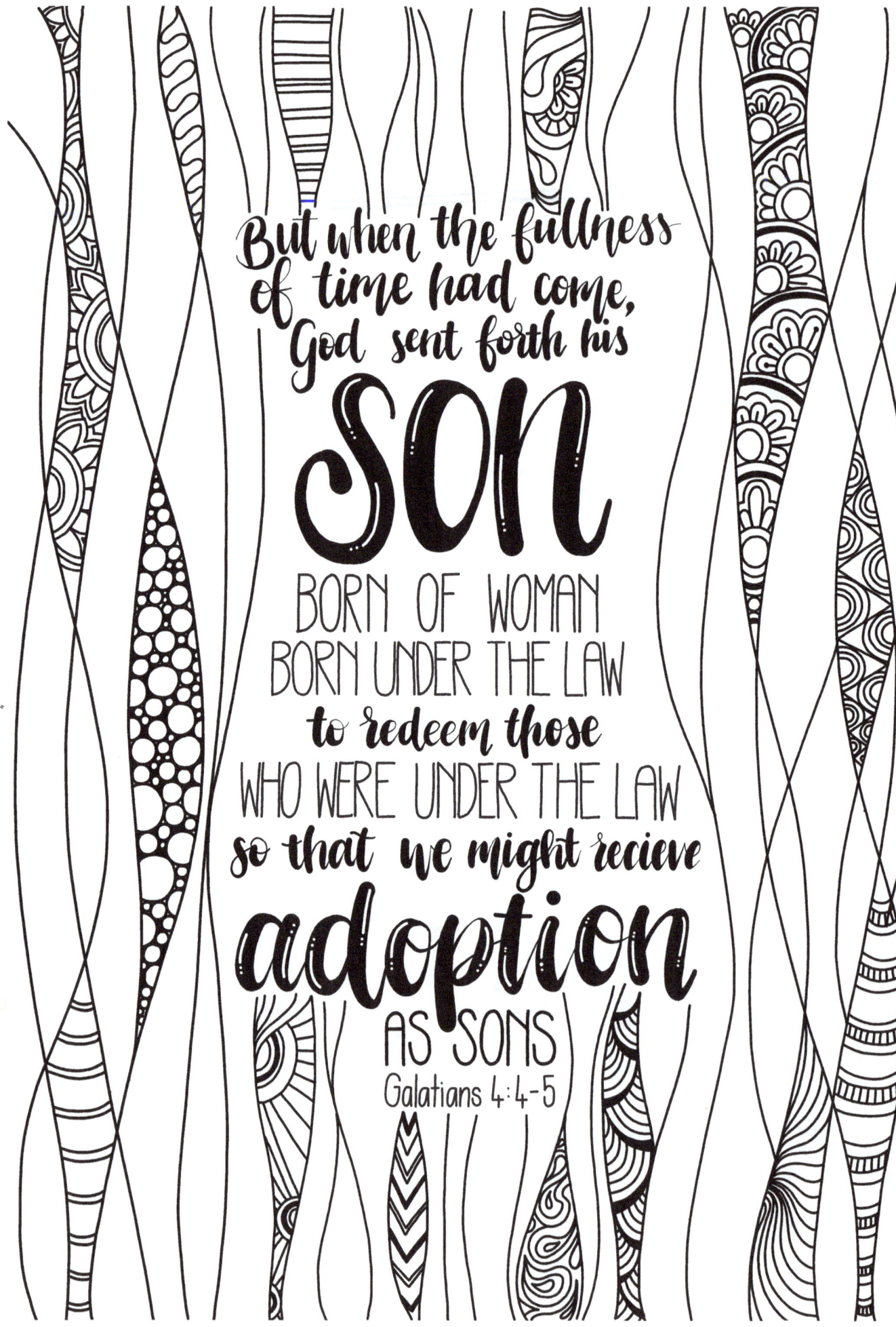

But when the fullness of time had come, God sent forth his SON BORN OF WOMAN BORN UNDER THE LAW to redeem those WHO WERE UNDER THE LAW so that we might recieve adoption AS SONS

Galatians 4:4-5

42

'Fullness of time'
www.firewheelpress.com

Pictures of your friends

1 Month Ahead

Practical

THINK

☐ Make a list of the things you want to do in the first week after you arrive.
☐ What are the cultural norms in the place to which you are moving?
☐ What are the road safety rules?

DECIDE

☐ Are there still goodbyes you want to say?
☐ Make a plan for emergency situations.
☐ Is there anything you want to take back with you that you need to buy?

Heart

SHARE

☐ What are the emotions you are feeling at this moment?
☐ Is there anything you are concerned about ?
☐ What are you looking forward to?

DISCUSS

☐ Make a goal list for your life transition?
☐ What is your plan for maintaining boundaries?

TO DO:

☐

☐

☐

☐

☐

☐

☐

☐

MOOD TRACKER

☐ Week 1

☐ Week 2

☐ Week 3

☐ Week 4

THOUGHTS AND PLANS

_____

_____

_____

_____

_____

_____

_____

_____

_____

_____

_____

REFLECTION

Launching into adulthood is a big thing and this is coming for you. Many of you are leaving your homes and your people. Many of you are leaving your homes, your people, and the rules in which you have lived in, and are entering into a world that is totally different to what you have seen before.

Galatians 3:26 relates to this back in the Roman days young people coming into adulthood would lay aside their childhood robe and put on a new toga. This represented the move into adulthood with full rights and responsibilities. What are some of the things you are going to need to be aware of as you move back into the next part of your journey? What does it mean for you to step into adulthood in your faith journey? Do you feel you are ready to be launched into adulthood.

It's okay to feel like you aren't ready. Some people may think you know what you are doing because of the life you have lived or the labels you carry. God is under no illusions. He knows where you are and he is here for you where you are.

BIBLE PASSAGE

GALATIANS 3:23-4:3

23 Now before faith came we were held in custody under the law, being kept as prisoners until the coming faith would be revealed. 24 Thus the law had become our guardian until Christ, so that we could be declared righteous by faith. 25 But now that faith has come, we are no longer under a guardian. 26 For in Christ Jesus you are all sons of God through faith. 27 For all of you who were baptised into Christ have clothed yourselves with Christ. 28 There is neither Jew nor Greek, there is neither slave nor free, there is neither male nor female—for all of you are one in Christ Jesus. 29 And if you belong to Christ, then you are Abraham's descendants, heirs according to the promise.

4 Now I mean that the heir, as long as he is a minor, is no different from a slave, though he is the owner of everything. 2 But he is under guardians and managers until the date set by his father. 3 So also we, when we were minors, were enslaved under the basic forces of the world.

QUESTIONS

• What was the purpose of the law (Torah)?

• Who is this written to?

• How does this illustration affect your understanding of the New Testament?

NOTES:

A copy of currency

Pictures of iconic/comical signs/ Cultural things

1 Week Ahead

Practical

THINK

☐ What do you need to do in the last week?
☐ Who are the people to whom you need to say goodbye?
☐ Make a list of things to pack.

DECIDE

☐ Start packing, weigh your luggage.
☐ What is the last meal you want to eat?

Heart

SHARE

☐ Breathe.
☐ How are you feeling?
☐ What are you concerned about?
☐ What are you looking forward to?

DISCUSS

☐ What have been your best memories in this location?
☐ What treasures are you taking with you?

TO DO:

☐
☐
☐
☐
☐
☐
☐
☐

MOOD TRACKER

☐ Day 1

☐ Day 2

☐ Day 3

☐ Day 4

☐ Day 5

☐ Day 6

☐ Day 7

THOUGHTS AND PLANS

_____

_____

_____

_____

_____

_____

_____

_____

_____

_____

_____

REFLECTION

As a TCK, you may feel you are put on a pedestal, that every time you go back to your passport country you are paraded in front of churches and people saying this is who you are. You feel the label on you. You sometimes feel you don't belong in one circle or another. But Paul in his writings talks about a different sort of belonging; he talks about being a child of God. He uses the image of being released from slavery to show that Christ came and died for you. You are invited into his story to have a relationship with him. He doesn't care what you have done, he cares about you. He has made a way to set you free from the laws and expectations that you have carried.

BIBLE PASSAGE

GALATIANS 4:4-11

But when the appropriate time had come, God sent out his Son, born of a woman, born under the law, 5 to redeem those who were under the law, so that we may be adopted as sons with full rights. 6 And because you are sons, God sent the Spirit of his Son into our hearts, who calls "Abba! Father!" 7 So you are no longer a slave but a son, and if you are a son, then you are also an heir through God.

Heirs of Promise Are Not to Return to Law
8 Formerly when you did not know God, you were enslaved to beings that by nature are not gods at all. 9 But now that you have come to know God (or rather to be known by God), how can you turn back again to the weak and worthless basic forces? Do you want to be enslaved to them all over again? 10 You are observing religious days and months and seasons and years. 11 I fear for you that my work for you may have been in vain.

QUESTIONS

• What does it mean to be a child of God?

• Are there things in your life to which you feel you are 'a slave'?

• Do you feel like you need to earn God's favour?

NOTES:

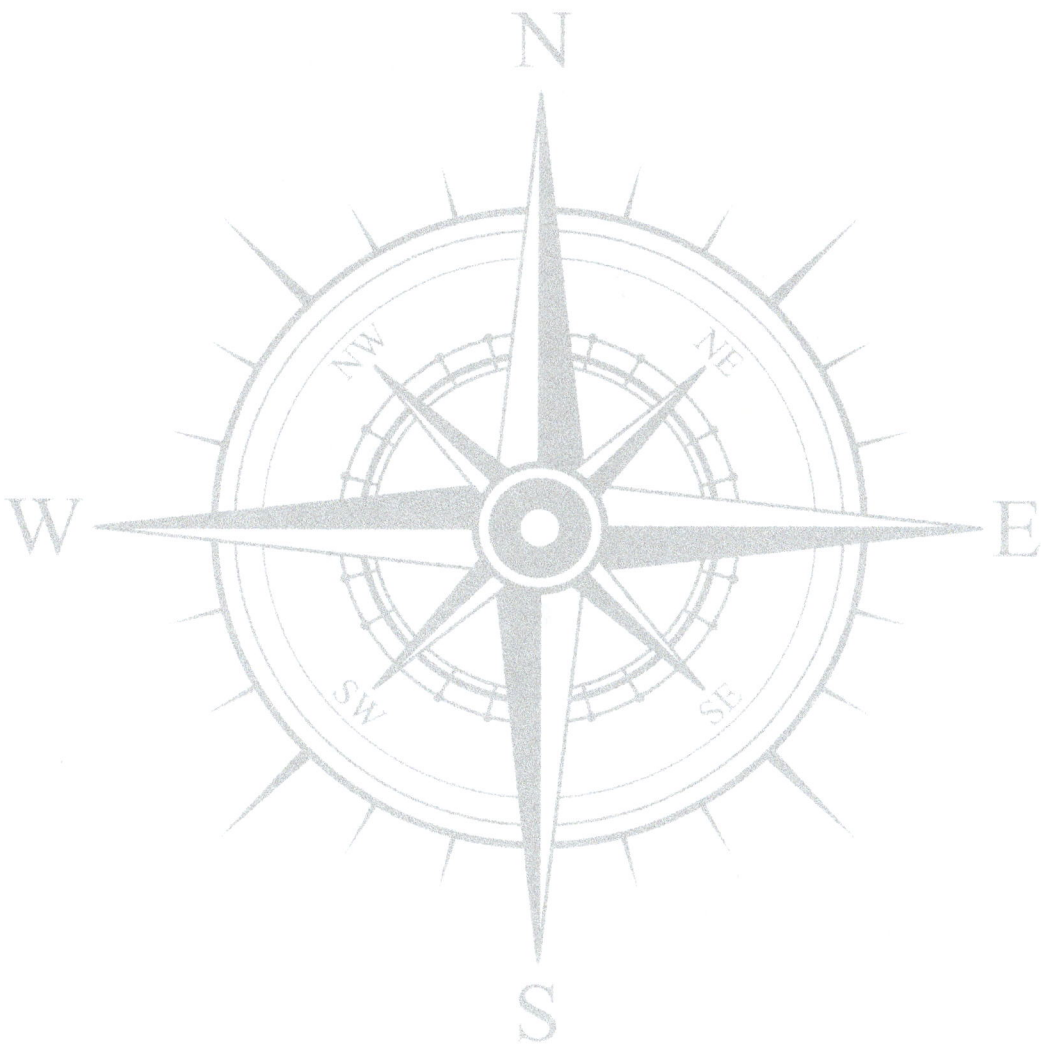

Create a map of where you currently live ?

Collect photos of the people you want to remember & write what you value about this person.

Travel

REFLECTION

You are on your way. How are you feeling? Is this good, exciting, scary, devastating, all of the above. It's okay to feel whatever you feel right now. There is no right way to feel right now. God is with you in whatever you are experiencing.

You are moving from one place to another, but wherever you go you always take yourself with you. There may be changes in and around you, but this moment right here is a chance for you to ask yourself what things you want to hold onto in the midst of change. What things or labels are you letting go of? What things do you wish you could let go of, but are finding it hard?

This passage points out that it's not about work, it's about faith. Some people will say that you should gain more knowledge, comprehend theology and memorise the bible. Being a follower of Christ is not about that. Christ asks us to live in relationship with him and as we learn truths about who he is and what he says about us we can hold onto them as consistent no matter our context.

So much may be changing, but God's love for you and willingness to walk with you through the messiness of life remains the same yesterday, today, and tomorrow.

BIBLE PASSAGE

GALATIANS 4:12-18

2 I beg you, brothers and sisters, become like me, because I have become like you. You have done me no wrong!

Personal Appeal of Paul
13 But you know it was because of a physical illness that I first proclaimed the gospel to you, 14 and though my physical condition put you to the test, you did not despise or reject me. Instead, you welcomed me as though I were an angel of God, as though I were Christ Jesus himself! 15 Where then is your sense of happiness now? For I testify about you that if it were possible, you would have pulled out your eyes and given them to me! 16 So then, have I become your enemy by telling you the truth?

17 They court you eagerly, but for no good purpose; they want to exclude you, so that you would seek them eagerly. 18 However, it is good to be sought eagerly for a good purpose at all times, and not only when I am present with you.

How have the people of God accepted you?

THOUGHTS AND PLANS

_____

_____

_____

_____

_____

_____

_____

_____

_____

_____

MOOD TRACKER

☐ Day 1

☐ Day 2

☐ Day 3

☐ Day 4

☐ Day 5

☐ Day 6

☐ Day 7

let us not grow weary of doing good for in due season we will reap if we do not give up.

Galatians 6:9

'Due Season'

www.firewheelpress.com

Airport Bingo

Play bingo at the airport add four more squares what you are on the lookout for.

Parent Trying to control child	Someone running late for their plane	Someone saying goodbye to someone	A pilot	A flight Attendant
Someone taking a photo of a plane	Someone taking selfies	Business person	Massage chair	Person with more than one device plugged in
Someone reading a book	Someone sleeping	Duty free shopping	Someone having to take shoes off	Someone having a video call
Drinking coffee	Someone taking more then one chair	Someone with heaps of luggage	Follow me vehicle	Luggage cart
Someone singing	Security checkpoint	Someone wearing sporting clothes	Someone wearing a mask	Someone repacking a suitcase

1 Week After

Practical

THINK

- ☐ Take time to adjust. Give yourself grace and know your boundaries.
- ☐ Talk to your bridging person.
- ☐ What routines do you want in your life? E.g. meals, exercise, church

DECIDE

- ☐ Do you need a driver's licence?
- ☐ Do you need to set up communications? E.g. phone, internet

Heart

SHARE

- ☐ What have you enjoyed so far?
- ☐ What has been the hardest part?
- ☐ What are you looking forward to?

DISCUSS

- ☐ What are you missing?
- ☐ How is the jet-lag effecting you?
- ☐ Mark where you sit currently on the river diagram.

TO DO:

- ☐
- ☐
- ☐
- ☐
- ☐
- ☐
- ☐

MOOD TRACKER

- ☐ Day 1
- ☐ Day 2
- ☐ Day 3
- ☐ Day 4
- ☐ Day 5
- ☐ Day 6
- ☐ Day 7

THOUGHTS AND PLANS

_____

_____

_____

_____

_____

_____

_____

_____

_____

_____

_____

_____

REFLECTION

Have you had a rough week? How are you feeling? Have you experienced jet-lag? There is so much happening right now and you may not have the bandwidth to pore over deep and challenging thoughts. That's okay.

Things don't all happen in the time frame and way that you may feel they should. Just like in this passage where Abraham got tried of waiting for God's way and so put Hagar and Ishmael in an impossible position, it can be hard to wait on God.

In the midst of your 1st week of adjustment, do you have space for meeting with God? Is there space for His voice and peace in your life?

BIBLE PASSAGE

GALATIANS 4:19-31

My children—I am again undergoing birth pains until Christ is formed in you! 20 I wish I could be with you now and change my tone of voice, because I am perplexed about you.

An Appeal from Allegory
21 Tell me, you who want to be under the law, do you not understand the law? 22 For it is written that Abraham had two sons, one by the slave woman and the other by the free woman. 23 But one, the son by the slave woman, was born by natural descent, while the other, the son by the free woman, was born through the promise. 24 These things may be treated as an allegory, for these women represent two covenants. One is from Mount Sinai bearing children for slavery; this is Hagar. 25 Now Hagar represents Mount Sinai in Arabia and corresponds to the present Jerusalem, for she is in slavery with her children. 26 But the Jerusalem above is free, and she is our mother. 27 For it is written:

"Rejoice, O barren woman who does not bear children;

Break forth and shout, you who have no birth pains, because the children of the desolate woman are more numerous When big changes in life hit, life gets overwhelming. There is a flood of unfamiliarity, and in the midst of that chaos we have to make decisions – often life-changing decisions. These seasons of transition are stressful, uncomfortable, and quite often turning points we'll look back on.

QUESTIONS

• Why is God's timing so important?

• Are you giving people you respect a voice in your life?

• Do you have people close to you who can help you navigate confusion in your faith?

NOTES:

1 Month After

Practical

THINK

- [ ] What things can you do to get to know this place?
- [ ] With whom you are connecting?
- [ ] What church do you want to be part of?

DECIDE

- [ ] What can you do to start making friends and find new activities?
- [ ] Do you need to write a resume?

Heart

SHARE

- [ ] What have you enjoyed so far?
- [ ] What are you missing?
- [ ] What has been the hardest part?
- [ ] Have you been able to share your story?

DISCUSS

- [ ] How has sharing your story affected you?
- [ ] What expectations are you bringing with your from your previous context?

TO DO:

- [ ]
- [ ]
- [ ]
- [ ]
- [ ]
- [ ]
- [ ]
- [ ]

MOOD TRACKER

- [ ] Week 1
- [ ] Week 2
- [ ] Week 3
- [ ] Week 4
- [ ] Week 5
- [ ] Week 6
- [ ] Week 7
- [ ] Week 8

THOUGHTS AND PLANS

_____

_____

_____

_____

_____

_____

_____

_____

_____

_____

_____

REFLECTION

How do you feel you are measuring up? What are the measures that you are applying to yourself? What others have done or said? What your parents have wanted of you? What do you feel like you are supposed to show to the world around you? How about the times when you realise that you are falling short of those measures? When you feel like there is no way to attain the goals that have been set?

But the race that God has called us into is not something that we run alone. God is one who is alongside us as well as fellow believers. When we feel like we are failing or are worried about what we should believe in or do, we can trust God to be the guide in confusing situations. We can also turn to those in our lives who are also in the journey of following God and share wisdom and learning together. Do you have someone that you are able to talk to about things that are frustrating or confusing?

BIBLE PASSAGE

GALATIANS 5:1-15

5 For freedom Christ has set us free. Stand firm, then, and do not be subject again to the yoke of slavery. 2 Listen! I, Paul, tell you that if you let yourselves be circumcised, Christ will be of no benefit to you at all! 3 And I testify again to every man who lets himself be circumcised that he is obligated to obey the whole law. 4 You who are trying to be declared righteous by the law have been alienated from Christ; you have fallen away from grace! 5 For through the Spirit, by faith, we wait expectantly for the hope of righteousness. 6 For in Christ Jesus neither circumcision nor uncircumcised carries any weight—the only thing that matters is faith working through love.

7 You were running well; who prevented you from obeying the truth? 8 This persuasion does not come from the one who calls you! 9 A little yeast makes the whole batch of dough rise! 10 I am confident in the Lord that you will accept no other view. But the one who is confusing you will pay the penalty, whoever he may be. 11 Now, brothers and sisters, if I am still preaching circumcision, why am I still being persecuted? In that case the offense of the cross has been removed. 12 I wish those agitators would go so far as to castrate themselves!

Practice Love
13 For you were called to freedom, brothers and sisters; only do not use your freedom as an opportunity to indulge your flesh, but through love serve one another. 14 For the whole law can be summed up in a single commandment, namely, "You must love your neighbour as yourself." 15 However, if you continually bite and devour one another, beware that you are not consumed by one another.

QUESTION

• What are some things you have believed and later found out were wrong?

• How can the cross of Christ be offensive?

• How does serving one another in love change a conflict?

NOTES:

Wreck this page

Photos of family before and after

3 Months After

Practical

THINK

- ☐ How well are you connecting with people?
- ☐ What new activities have you found?

DECIDE

- ☐ How ready are you to invest in new relationships?
- ☐ Is your financial plan working?

Heart

SHARE

- ☐ What is the best thing so far?
- ☐ What has been the hardest thing so far?
- ☐ What are you looking forward to?
- ☐ What are you missing?

DISCUSS

- ☐ What has surprised you since moving?
- ☐ What has matched your expectations?

TO DO:

- ☐
- ☐
- ☐
- ☐
- ☐
- ☐
- ☐

Mood Tracker

- ☐ Week 1
- ☐ Week 2
- ☐ Week 3
- ☐ Week 4
- ☐ Week 5
- ☐ Week 6
- ☐ Week 7
- ☐ Week 8
- ☐ Week 9
- ☐ Week 10
- ☐ Week 11
- ☐ Week 12

THOUGHTS AND PLANS

_____

_____

_____

_____

_____

_____

_____

_____

_____

_____

_____

_____

REFLECTION

It has been 3 months in your new place. How is it going? Have there been things that have shocked or frustrated you? What were some things you weren't expecting? Things from within you and things around you?

This passage can almost feel like a complete turn around from what Paul has been talking about. Grace instead of law and freedom instead of slavery. But here it almost seems like a new set of rules: things you should or should not do in order to make God happy.

But it is important to remember that everything that has already been said up to this point remains true. God is still calling you to his grace and freedom. What you have here is a description of what it looks like when you allow the Spirit to work in your life. These are not tasks you need to avoid or achieve, but when you allow the Spirit to move in your life what is produced will be of the Spirit. Your dependence is still completely on God and not on you to transform your life.

BIBLE PASSAGE

GALATIANS 5:16-26

But I say, live by the Spirit and you will not carry out the desires of the flesh. 17 For the flesh has desires that are opposed to the Spirit, and the Spirit has desires that are opposed to the flesh, for these are in opposition to each other, so that you cannot do what you want.

18 But if you are led by the Spirit, you are not under the law. 19 Now the works of the flesh are obvious: sexual immorality, impurity, depravity, 20 idolatry, sorcery, hostilities, strife, jealousy, outbursts of anger, selfish rivalries, dissensions, factions, 21 envying, murder, drunkenness, carousing, and similar things. I am warning you, as I had warned you before: Those who practice such things will not inherit the kingdom of God!

22 But the fruit of the Spirit is love, joy, peace, patience, kindness, goodness, faithfulness, 23 gentleness, and self-control. Against such things there is no law. 24 Now those who belong to Christ have crucified the flesh with its passions and desires. 25 If we live by the Spirit, let us also behave in accordance with the Spirit. 26 Let us not become conceited, provoking one another, being jealous of one another.

QUESTIONS

• How do you know the difference between the desires of the sinful nature and the direction of the Spirit?

• Where have you seen these fruit?

• How does following the Holy Spirit change relationships?

Create a map of your new location

Photos of life at the moment and how you feel about it.

6 Months After

Practical

THINK

- [ ] What have been worthwhile activities since you arrived?
- [ ] Do you have quality people around you?
- [ ] Are you enjoying yourself?
- [ ] What is your spiritual life like?

DECIDE

- [ ] Are there any changes you need to make to your current habits?
- [ ] Are there new things you want to start?

Heart

SHARE

- [ ] What is the best thing so far?
- [ ] What has been the hardest thing so far?
- [ ] What are you looking forward to?
- [ ] What are you missing?

DISCUSS

- [ ] Mark where you currently sit on the river diagram.
- [ ] How are you doing with the move?

TO DO:

- [ ]
- [ ]
- [ ]
- [ ]
- [ ]
- [ ]
- [ ]
- [ ]

MOOD TRACKER

- [ ] Week 1
- [ ] Week 2
- [ ] Week 3
- [ ] Week 4
- [ ] Week 5
- [ ] Week 6
- [ ] Week 7
- [ ] Week 8
- [ ] Week 9
- [ ] Week 10
- [ ] Week 11
- [ ] Week 12

THOUGHTS AND PLANS

_____

_____

_____

_____

_____

_____

_____

_____

_____

_____

_____

REFLECTION

What does it mean to 'plant' things in your life? Does it happen fast or slow? Is it like building friendships or trying again when things haven't worked? What about walking away from connections that tear you down instead of building you up? What can you see being planted in your life? What do you want there and what do you want to remove?

Just remember that real growth is slow. Sometimes the best things take ages to grow to maturity.

BIBLE PASSAGE

GALATIANS 6:1-5

Brothers and sisters, if a person is discovered in some sin, you who are spiritual restore such a person in a spirit of gentleness. Pay close attention to yourselves, so that you are not tempted too. 2 Carry one another's burdens, and in this way you will fulfil the law of Christ. 3 For if anyone thinks he is something when he is nothing, he deceives himself. 4 Let each one examine his own work. Then he can take pride in himself and not compare himself with someone else. 5 For each one will carry his own load.

QUESTIONS

• Who do you compare yourself with?

• What does it mean to share a burden?

NOTES:

Favourite new restaurants and food

Wreck this page

9 Months After

Practical

THINK

- [ ] Where do you have input into your community?
- [ ] Who are your support people?

DECIDE

- [ ] To what degree can you invest in your friends from your previous location?
- [ ] Do you need more supportive people close to you?

Heart

SHARE

- [ ] What is the best thing so far?
- [ ] What has been the hardest thing so far?
- [ ] What are you looking forward to?
- [ ] What are you missing?

DISCUSS

- [ ] Where is your heart?
- [ ] What can you contribute to the place in which you are now living?
- [ ] What do you want out of the place in which you are now living?

TO DO:

- [ ]
- [ ]
- [ ]
- [ ]
- [ ]
- [ ]
- [ ]
- [ ]

MOOD TRACKER

- [ ] Week 1
- [ ] Week 2
- [ ] Week 3
- [ ] Week 4
- [ ] Week 5
- [ ] Week 6
- [ ] Week 7
- [ ] Week 8
- [ ] Week 9
- [ ] Week 10
- [ ] Week 11
- [ ] Week 12

THOUGHTS AND PLANS

REFLECTION

Do you have beliefs that you are passionately holding on to? Are they beliefs that bring life to you and your community? Are they beliefs that bring conflict? Have you examined where these beliefs are rooted and where God meets you in this conversation?

Are you holding to the truth of Christ and the work of the Spirit in your life or are you holding to traditions and practices that give power to some over others?

If so, what do you need to hear from God to know that path forward? Ask him. He is listening and is faithful and forgiving. The work that he has begun in you he will carry on to completion. (Philippians 1:6)

BIBLE PASSAGE

GALATIANS 6:6-14

Now the one who receives instruction in the word must share all good things with the one who teaches it. 7 Do not be deceived. God will not be made a fool. For a person will reap what he sows, 8 because the person who sows to his own flesh will reap corruption from the flesh, but the one who sows to the Spirit will reap eternal life from the Spirit. 9 So we must not grow weary in doing good, for in due time we will reap, if we do not give up. 10 So then, whenever we have an opportunity, let us do good to all people, and especially to those who belong to the family of faith.

Final Instructions and Benediction
11 See what big letters I make as I write to you with my own hand!

12 Those who want to make a good showing in external matters are trying to force you to be circumcised. They do so only to avoid being persecuted for the cross of Christ. 13 For those who are circumcised do not obey the law themselves, but they want you to be circumcised so that they can boast about your flesh. 14 But may I never boast except in the cross of our Lord Jesus Christ, through which the world has been crucified to me, and I to the world

QUESTIONS

• What does it mean to boast in Christ?

• What are you planting in your life now that you will harvest later?

NOTES:

NAVIGATING GLOBAL TRANSITION AGAIN

Design by Zeborah Grace

Wreck this page

12 Months After

Practical

THINK

☐ How do you feel about the journey you have been on?
☐ Do you feel connected to this community?

DECIDE

☐ Are there changes you need to make?
☐ What is your plan for making those changes?

Heart

SHARE

☐ What is the best thing so far?
☐ What has been the hardest thing so far?
☐ What are you looking forward to?
☐ What are you missing?

DISCUSS

☐ Talk with someone about what these 24 months have been like.
☐ Mark where you sit on the river diagram.
☐ How do you see yourself within the Church?

TO DO:

☐

☐

☐

☐

☐

☐

☐

MOOD TRACKER

☐ Week 1
☐ Week 2
☐ Week 3
☐ Week 4
☐ Week 5
☐ Week 6
☐ Week 7
☐ Week 8
☐ Week 9
☐ Week 10
☐ Week 11
☐ Week 12

THOUGHTS AND PLANS

_____

_____

_____

_____

_____

_____

_____

_____

_____

_____

_____

REFLECTION

It's been a year. How about that!

What have been the significant changes for you this year?

Are there things that used to matter to you that don't any more? Or things that didn't matter that do now?

Looking back over the last two years how has your understanding of transformation changed? What do you know now that you wish you could share with yourself when you started this journey? Take some time to share these things with a friend. Growth is not a straight and steady line, but a winding journey where you need to take encouragement along the way. God is not finished. This is a season of your journey and he has much still in store for you.

May you be blessed with a heart and mind that are ready to learn and be transformed as you also bring others along on the journey.

Thank you for doing this journey with us.

Feel free to reach out and let us know how you went.

Cheers!

BIBLE PASSAGE

GALATIANS 6:15-18

For neither circumcision nor uncircumcised counts for anything; the only thing that matters is a new creation! 16 And all who will behave in accordance with this rule, peace and mercy be on them, and on the Israel of God.

17 From now on let no one cause me trouble, for I bear the marks of Jesus on my body.

18 The grace of our Lord Jesus Christ be with your spirit, brothers and sisters. Amen.

QUESTION

• How can his scars show that Paul belongs to Jesus?

• What does it mean to be a new creation?

NOTES:

Favourite new phrases and slang

Favourite places

Glossary

USE THIS TO WRITE YOUR OWN LANGUAGE FAVOURITE WORDS
AND MEANINGS WITH YOUR FRIENDS AND FAMILY.

Resources

BOOKS

• Misunderstood: The Impact of Growing Up Overseas in the 21st Century – Tanya Crossman (Summertime Publishing, 2016).
• Third Culture Kids: Growing Up Among Worlds (3rd Edition) – David Pollock, Ruth Van Reken, Michael Pollock (Nicholas Brealey Publishing, 2017).
• Belonging Everywhere and Nowhere: Insights into Counselling the Globally Mobile – Lois Bushong (Mango Tree Intercultural Services, 2013).
• Third Culture Kids: A Gift to Care For – Ulrika Ernvik (Familjeglädje, 2018).
• Expat Teens Talk: Peers, Parents and Professionals offer support, advice and solutions in response to Expat Life challenges as shared by Expat Teens – Lisa Pittman and Diana Smit (Summertime Publishing, 2012).
• The Global Nomad's Guide to University Transition, 2nd Ed. – Tina Quick (Tina L Quick, 2022).
• The Re-entry Roadmap: Find Your Best Next Step After Living Abroad – Cate Brubaker (Thinking Travel Press, 2018).
• Arriving Well – Cate Brubaker, Doreen Cumberford, Helen Watts (Kindle Direct Publishing, 2018).
• The Art of Coming Home – Craig Storti (Nicholas Brealey Publishing, 2001).
• Looming Transitions – Amy Young (CreateSpace Independent Publishing Platform, 2015).
• Returning Well: Your Guide to Thriving Back "Home" After Serving Cross-Culturally – Melissa Chaplin (Newton Publishers, 2015).
• Burn-Up or Splash Down: surviving the culture shock of re-entry – Marion Knell (IVP Books, 2007).
• Re-Entry: Making The Transition From Missions To Life At Home – Peter Jordan (YWAM, 2013).
• Unstacking Your Grief Tower – Lauren Wells (Independently published, 2021).
• Belonging Beyond Borders – Megan Norton (Belonging Beyond Borders LLC, 2022).
• Between Worlds: Essays on Culture and Belonging – Marilyn Gardner (Doorlight Publications, 2015).
• Worlds Apart: A Third Culture Kid's Journey – Marilyn Gardner (Doorlight Publications, 2018)

www.ingramcontent.com/pod-product-compliance
Lightning Source LLC
Chambersburg PA
CBHW080858030426

42334CB00022B/2624